Animal Activities
Animals Eating

JANE BURTON

Belitha Press

First published in Great Britain in 1990 by
Belitha Press Limited
31 Newington Green, London N16 9PU
Text copyright © Jane Burton 1990
Photographs copyright © Jane Burton and
Kim Taylor 1990
Editor/Art Director: Treld Bicknell
All rights reserved. No part of this book
may be reproduced or utilized in any form or
by any means, electronic or mechanical,
including photocopying, recording or by
any information storage and retrieval
system, without permission in writing from
the Publisher.

Printed in the UK for Imago Publishing

British Library Cataloguing in Publication Data

Burton, Jane, *1933*-
  Eating
  1. Animals. Behaviour – For children
  I. Title   II. Series
  591.51

ISBN 0 947553 88 6

The first food that any mammal gets is milk. As soon as a baby is born, it finds one of its mother's teats and starts to suck. Milk is rich, and the baby grows fast.

◀ These puppies are a month old and big enough to reach their mother's teats while she is standing. The Kongoni calf is *so* big that it has to kneel ▲ while it suckles. Soon these babies will stop suckling. The puppies will gobble meat, and the calf will graze grass.

◀ Town mice are not fussy, they eat whatever they can find. These House Mice are dining on cat food. But the ginger tom on the cat food packet looks as if *he* wants to eat the mice!

Country mice eat mostly seeds. Harvest Mice ▲ climb wheat stalks to nibble the ripe grain. Their tails help them to hold on while they use their front paws as hands.

All mice have special front teeth for gnawing hard foods such as seeds. Cats have quite different teeth, pointed and sharp for catching and slicing meat – such as mice!

▼ Grass grows nearly everywhere, and all sorts of animals graze it. An Ostrich pecks new shoots that have sprung up after rain. He eats berries, leaves and insects, too – whatever he can find. When he has a mouthful, he lifts his head and swallows. You can see the lump of food as it slides down his throat.

Common Zebras eat *only* grass. They need to munch a lot of it, especially when it is old and tough and turned to hay in the hot sun. ▼

▼ The Gerenuk is a long-necked antelope that browses on leaves. This buck is daintily plucking them one at a time. When he has eaten all the best ones at nose level, he will stand up on his hind legs to reach the ones higher up.

An African Elephant picks leafy twigs with his trunk – a whole bunch at a time – and feeds them into his mouth. He can chew bark and hard fruits, as well as grasses so tough that even zebras cannot eat them. He has massive cheek teeth which can crush such woody food. ▼

A caterpillar *seems* to spend its whole life eating. But even caterpillars have to pause sometimes. Those of the Large White Butterfly have left themselves just enough nasturtium leaf for comfort.

The Elephant Hawk Moth caterpillar rests by day near the ground and climbs a fuchsia bush to feed at night. Most sorts of caterpillar eat only one or two sorts of leaf. The Puss Moth feeds mainly on the leaves of poplar or willow. When the caterpillars become butterflies and moths they don't really eat at all. They only sip nectar from flowers or juice from rotten fruit.

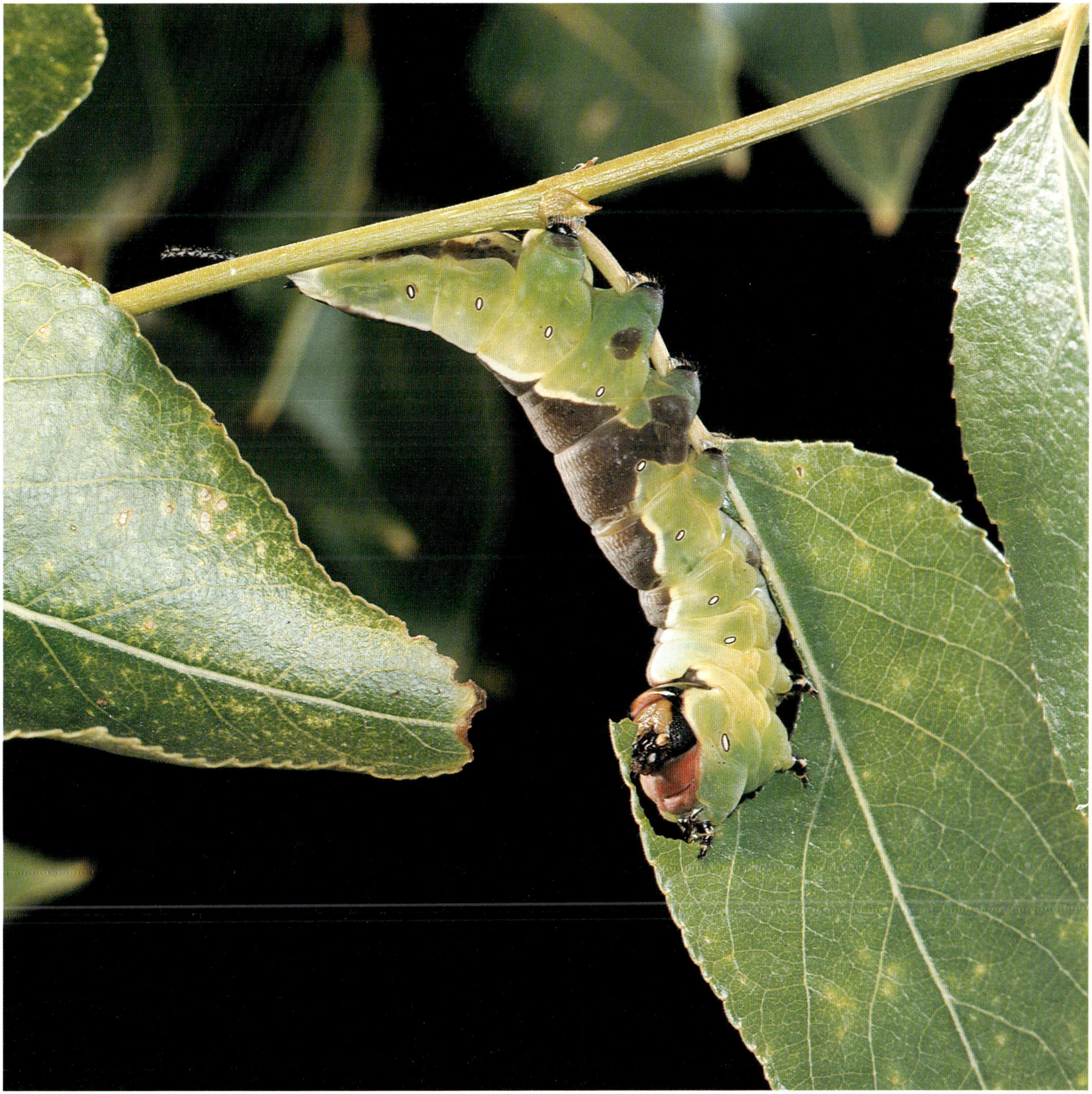

This Green Iguana looks like a fearsome dragon, but it is a harmless plant-eater. It spends most of its time climbing in trees, tasting a leaf here, a flower there. Sometimes it comes down for a swim in a forest pool and a meal of waterlily petals.

The Greek Tortoise could well have stalked the earth among armour-plated dinosaurs. But it, too, is a gentle vegetarian. Trampler, a pet tortoise, demolishes whole lettuces and other green vegetables, cutting out neat bites with his sharp jaws. In the summer he feasts, then fasts through the winter when salad plants are dead.

▲ Most reptiles eat insects. The High-casqued Chameleon has an amazingly long tongue to help him catch them. When a grasshopper comes within reach, this chameleon leans over, takes careful aim, then 'shoots' the grasshopper with his tongue. When the insect is caught, the chameleon flips his tongue back into his mouth, taking the grasshopper with it.

Amphibians are also insect-eaters. The European Tree Frog only has a short blob of a tongue. When it sees an insect alight within range, it shoots at it by launching its whole body and captures the damselfly – with a little tongue and big wide mouth. ▶

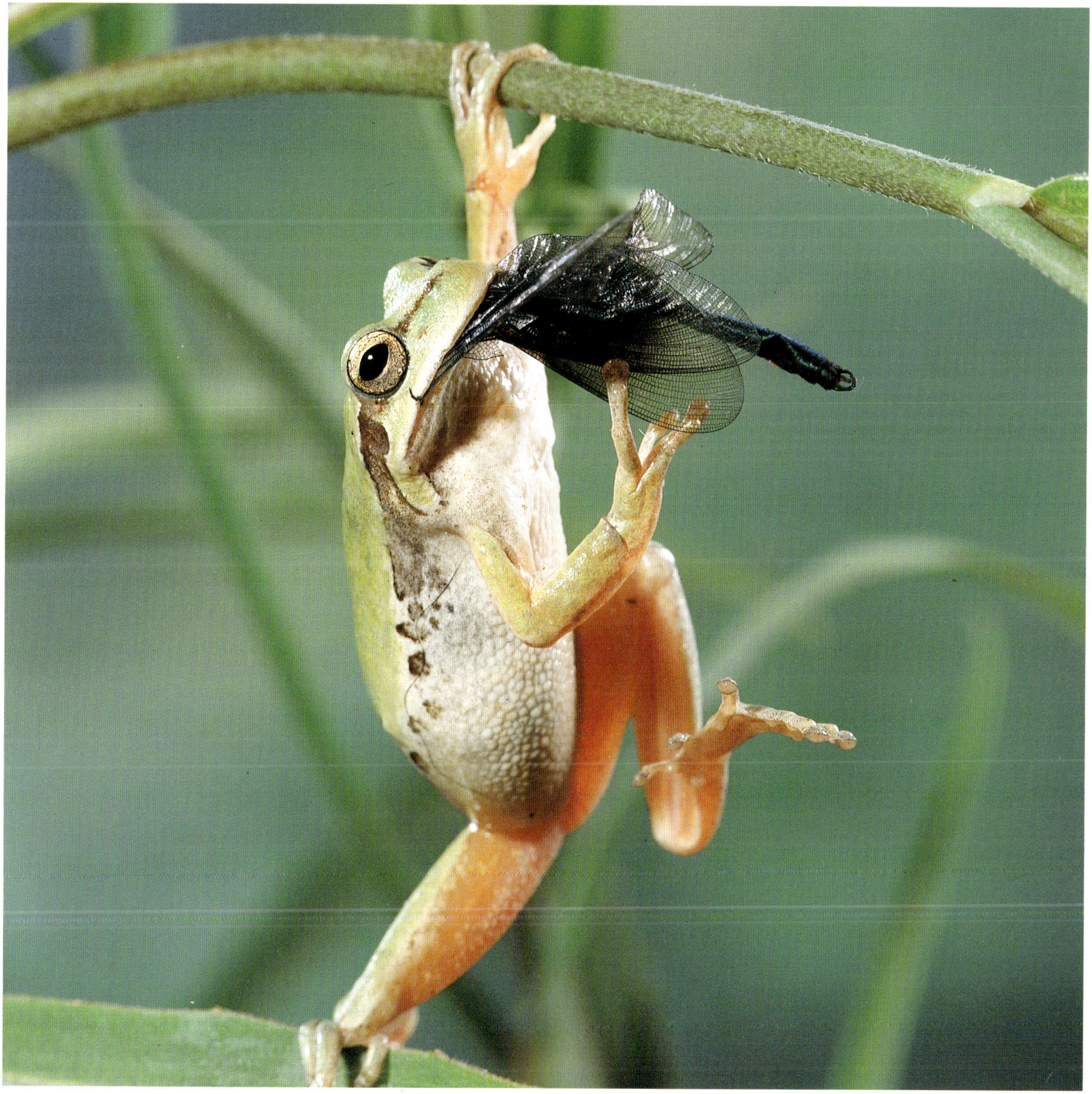

▲ The Painted Prawn feeds on starfish – with the co-operation of its victim! It snips away at a weak spot on one of the starfish's arms, while the starfish just sits there, helping to complete the break. When the arm has been cut through, the prawn carries it off to eat, while the starfish goes away and grows a new arm.

A Grass Snake feeds mainly on frogs, which it swallows whole. To get such a big meal down all in one go, the snake unhinges its lower jaw and stretches the skin of its throat. Its muscles work hard to ease the large frog down the snake's gullet. ▲

▲ All spiders are venomous. They kill their prey with a poisonous bite. This fat female Garden Spider lurks in the centre of her web, waiting for an insect to blunder into it. When a cranefly gets snared, she rushes over, bites it, then wraps it in silk. She will carry it away, to eat later.

The Raft Spider taps on the surface of the water with her foot, making little ripples as if a tiny insect had fallen in. A small fish darts over to snap up the insect, but instead *it* gets snapped up by the spider. ▲

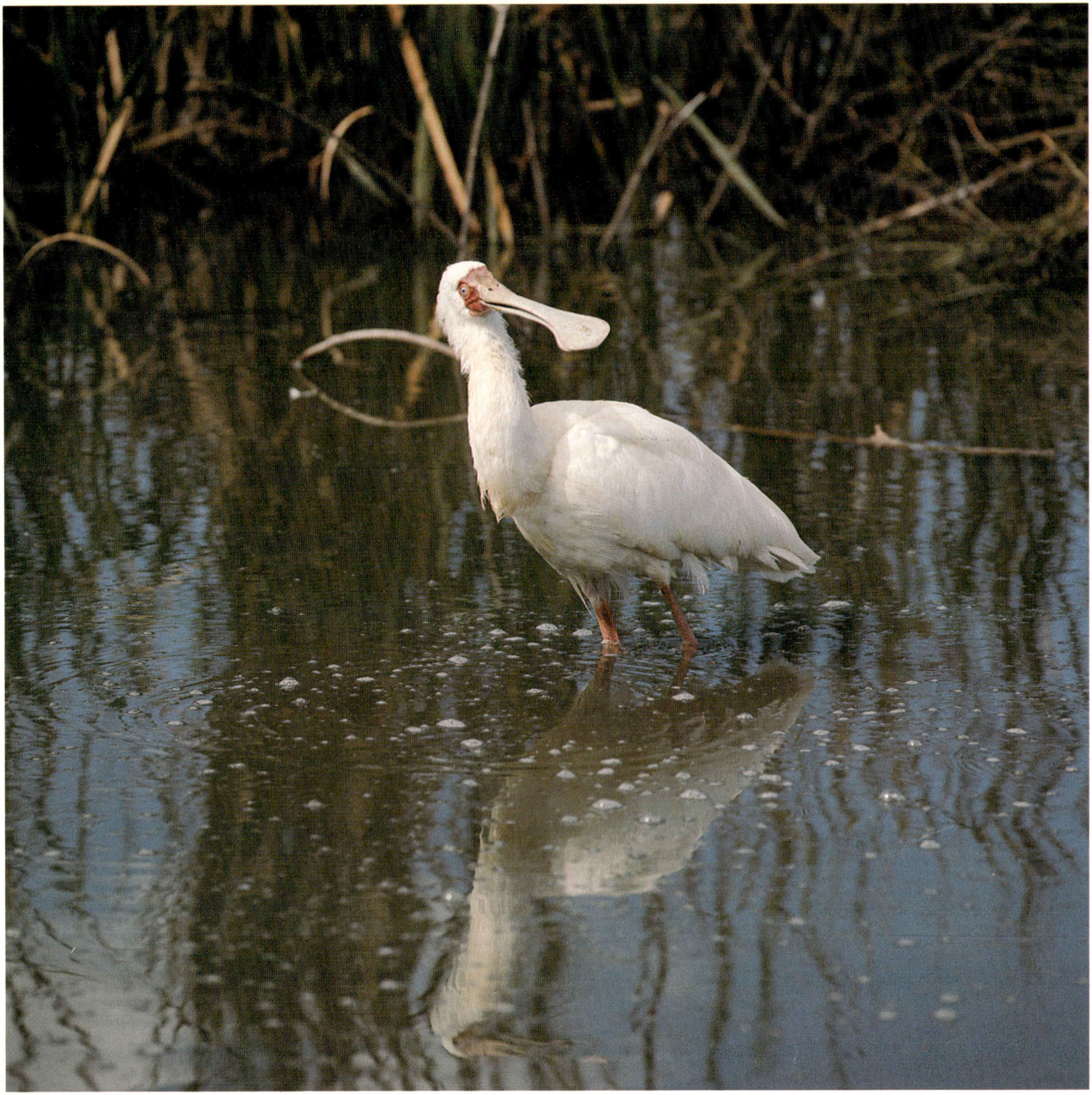

◀ Some birds have unusual beaks which help them catch food in special ways. The African Spoonbill hurries through shallow water, scooping from side to side with its beak. It can feel and catch little fishes or shrimps between the flat ends of its spoon-shaped bill.

▼ The Lesser Flamingo paddles more sedately, sieving tiny blue-green algae from the soupy water with its very special upsidedown beak.

White Pelicans all plunge their fishing-net beaks into the water together. Their pouches trap lots of water and a few fishes. The birds lift their heads out, the water drains away, and the fish are tossed back and swallowed. ▼

▲ The Freshwater Pufferfish has a sharp beak which can chop right through a shrimp's hard skin. But the Argus Fish has a tiny soft mouth so it waits until the puffer has finished feeding. Then the Argus daintily cleans up the left-overs. ▲

The Pike has long sharp teeth for catching and holding its prey. This young one has caught a Ten-spined Stickleback, but cannot swallow it. The 'stickle' has erected all its spines and is stuck in the Pike's mouth. The Pike will have to spit the stickle out if it can, and give up its meal this time.

▶

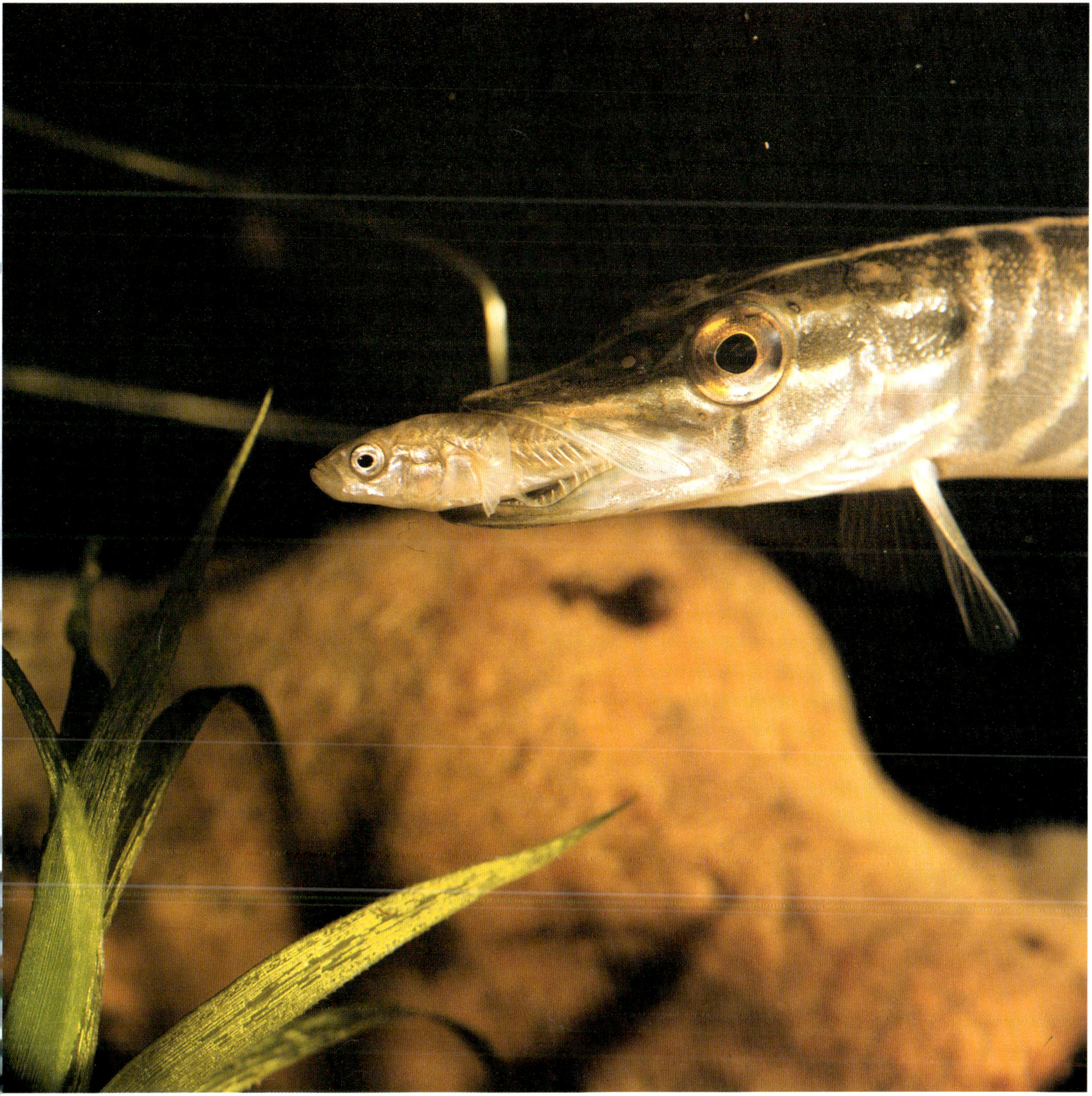

▼ Baby Tawny Owls sit on a branch waiting for one of their parents to bring them a mouse. They are big enough to swallow one whole, but it is hard work. The owlet jerks its head back and gulps, and looks quite uncomfortable, even after the mouse has disappeared inside. The smaller owlet will be able to grab the next mouse that is brought, now that big brother is too full to bother snatching it first.

The Grey Heron also has trouble gulping down the huge fish it has caught. Big prey must always be swallowed headfirst – the way it is streamlined – because it won't slide down – tailfirst or sideways! ▶

Moles and earthworms spend most of their lives tunnelling through the earth. The earthworms eat the earth and the moles eat the earthworms. A European Mole uses its spade-like hands to hold a worm down while eating it, so that grains of soil stuck on the slimy outside of the worm are rubbed off, and silt in the worm's gut is squeezed out – making the mole's dinner less gritty. A mole can eat nearly its own weight of worms in a day.

Almost every sort of animal risks being eaten by another larger animal. Grass-eaters are eaten by meat-eaters, meat-eaters are eaten by bigger meat-eaters. Only the biggest meat-eaters of all are safe.

During the night a lioness and her sisters have killed a zebra and shared the meat with their cubs. Now the others are sleeping off their feast, under a bush. She stays to guard the kill from vultures and hyenas. She herself will only fall prey to another animal after many years, when she becomes weakened by injury or old age.

This Golden Hamster lives in underground tunnels. She comes above ground at night to search for nuts and seeds, which she stuffs into her cheek pouches. When her cheeks are bulging, she toddles off to her nest. There she unpouches the nuts into her food store. In the wild, hamsters collect huge stores when there is plenty of food about, so that when food is scarce outside they still have enough to eat.